Terri,

Just a few inspirational words while up on "the hot tin roof." You are an inspiration to all of us at Otwell. Thank you for representing us all for such a great cause, Relay For Life. I know Alison's watching from heaven.

Be careful and don't get burned!

Doris

Published by Humble Creek, P.O. Box 719, Uhrichsville, Ohio 44683

ecpa Member of the
Evangelical Christian
Publishers Association

Printed in China.

Take Your Mark

Motivational Stories about Women of Achievement

Written and Compiled by
Angela Kiesling

HUMBLE CREEK
INSPIRATION FOR LIFE

God didn't put us here and give us dreams
and a heart to do things just to confuse us.
I believe He has a very specific plan
for each of our lives.

GINNY OWENS

GINNY
OWENS

Ginny held back the tears until she was safely inside her bedroom, away from the stares of the other kids. It was the same old awkwardness again—that "differentness" about her that kept people at arms' length and made her feel like a pariah. Even though a few of them tried to be kind, they couldn't seem to get past her blindness. At times the pain of polite rejection cut to the heart.

As always, she found solace through music and God.

"Growing up is always difficult," says Ginny, now in her midtwenties and a recording artist for Rocketown Records, a label founded by Christian pop singer Michael W. Smith. "All adolescents have growing pains. But when you realize you're different from other people, it really shocks you."

Born with poor eyesight, Ginny lost what little vision she had by the age of two. But at the same time she showed a precocious talent for the piano, singing, and picking out melodies while other little girls were learning to play patty-cake.

Her gift for music grew as the years passed, and a career as a music teacher seemed like an obvious choice. She attended Belmont University in Nashville—known for its strong music program—on a full scholarship and after graduation applied for a job at several schools. But the cum laude graduate discovered that principals were reluctant to employ her.

"They would be impressed with my resume, but when they met me, they would freak out and worry that hiring a blind person just wouldn't work," Ginny said in a newspaper interview.

During this time of career searching, Ginny met a Nashville music publisher who listened to her three-song demo tape and, on the basis of those three songs, brought her on board his song-writing staff. He later introduced her to producer Monroe Jones, who recalls that when he first heard Ginny play the piano and sing, "I couldn't believe my ears. By the chorus of the first song, I knew I wanted to work with her."

The two put together another demo tape and sent it to Rocketown Records, which in September 1998 signed Ginny to a recording contract. Her first album, *Without Condition,* released in July 1999 to critical acclaim. By late August, the album's first single, "Free," hit No. 1 on the Adult Contemporary Christian charts. Ginny also beat out three hundred other artists to win a spot on the Lilith Fair tour's Nashville lineup.

"Ginny has no pretense, and she's unstoppable," Jones once said about his protège. "We're talking about a girl who couldn't see, yet still ran track in high school. She lives on her own and even mows her own yard."

Though often troubled by people's reaction to her blindness, Ginny says she can see God's purpose in it. As she told *CCM Magazine* in August 1999, "It's like He takes the thing I like least about myself and uses it for His glory."

Throughout the years, whether facing hardship or mind-boggling successes, Ginny says God has taught her that He's the only reliable friend in the universe.

"It's so important to pursue a relationship with your Creator. God didn't put us here and give us dreams and a heart to do things just to confuse us. I believe He has a very specific plan for each of our lives. Always pursue the things that are important, and [the things] that you love to do."

I want you to know
that dreams do come true.
If they didn't,
why would God design our hearts
with the capacity to yearn for something
greater than ourselves?

HEATHER WHITESTONE

HEATHER
WHITESTONE

The opening quotation, written by Heather Whitestone—Miss America 1995—leaps off page two of her autobiography, *Listening with My Heart,* which tells the story of how her dream did come true, against formidable odds.

Though born with normal hearing, an early childhood illness left Heather deaf and so weak that she had to relearn how to walk. Doctors told her parents she would never develop beyond a third-grade education—let alone dance ballet or learn to speak.

Heather did both, and more.

Encouraged by her parents' belief in her potential, she worked long hours to master the skills of speech and enter the world of the hearing. Her mother enrolled her in dance classes, hoping that the disciplined training would improve her rhythm of speech.

Ironically, the one place Heather felt "just like everyone

else" was in the dance studio. "I loved everything about dancing!" she recalls in her autobiography. "For once I didn't have to talk to make my feelings known. . . . I was determined to be the best."

Dance became the place where her dreams could soar, and like other young girls she dreamed of twirling in the spotlight before a crowd—and winning a crown for her performance.

Determined to be remembered as something other than "the deaf girl" in her high school yearbook, Heather entered a local Junior Miss Pageant and came in second runner-up; she won the talent competition. After entering a series of other small pageants, she set her sights on the Miss Alabama Pageant in college.

On her first two trips to the Miss Alabama Pageant, she came in first runner-up—a title that, she recalls, "became my enemy." She was finally crowned the winner in 1994, and from that point on the only direction was up.

In Atlantic City for the Miss America Pageant 1995, Heather and the other contestants rehearsed for days before the final night of competition. During one rehearsal, she found herself staring at the "rehearsal crown," longing to touch it—despite the unspoken rule that contestants shouldn't touch the crown.

Yet, after they practiced "crowning" the stand-in winner during rehearsal, Heather reached out and helped the woman take the crown out of her hair.

"Oh, no," teased one of the hostesses standing by. "Whoever touches this crown will be the next Miss America."

"My heart beat faster as my head flooded with visions of what that crown could mean to me," Heather recalls. "That crown would give me a bigger voice to encourage people to follow the dreams God has given them. That crown would enlarge my witness for Jesus."

Though discouraged from using a Christian song for her talent segment, Heather chose to dance ballet to "Via Dolorosa," a song about the road Jesus walked to the cross. Later that night, as she was crowned Miss America 1995—the first Miss America with a disability—she turned to the applauding crowd and signed "I love you" with her right hand. As she writes in her book, "That night the sign had spread like a virus through the crowd. Almost everyone waved the 'I love you' sign back."

Looking back, I think God was gently, patiently tapping me on the shoulder and calling my name for years. But I continuously brushed Him off. It took total devastation before I would acquiesce and say, "OK, God. You can have my life."

MICHELLE AKERS

MICHELLE
AKERS

While 90,185 fans roared outside in the stadium, Michelle Akers lay flat on her back in the training room, nearly incoherent with fatigue. It was the 1999 Women's World Cup soccer tournament, her third and final World Cup, and yet there she lay with IVs dripping fluids into her veins.

"When I did gain my senses and learn that [a team player] had put away the winner, I had the trainers take my IVs out and found myself hobbling out to the field to join my team," recalls Michelle. "The fans were going crazy. I was struggling to soak it all in and keep myself together. It was incredible. I will never forget that moment."

The tournament proved to be more than a team victory; it was also a personal victory for Michelle. After a five-year struggle with Chronic Fatigue Syndrome, the thirty-three-year-old athlete had still managed to achieve her dream. "Knowing that I gave the team every ounce of effort I could muster was very satisfying for me. I simply left everything I had on the field."

Giving her all comes naturally to Michelle, but losing—especially to a strange illness—does not.

The typical tomboy, as a child Michelle sported a No. 75 "Mean Joe" Greene Pittsburgh Steelers jersey and had a fierce competitive streak. "I hated to lose," she remembers. "Even if I lost in Monopoly, I got mad."

Seeing her daughter's athletic bent, Michelle's mother signed her up to play soccer at age eight. But when the team lost repeatedly, Michelle begged to drop out. Her mother said no.

As time passed, she fell in love with the sport, and her skill on the soccer field matched her passion for the game. Michelle reached college age—in the early 1980s—at the same time women's soccer gained a foothold on many U.S. campuses. At the University of Central Florida in Orlando, she earned All-America honors four times and won the first women's Hermann Award as the nation's top player.

In 1985, word spread that U.S. Soccer was forming a women's national team. Michelle not only made the team, but went on to become its biggest scorer, leading Team USA to a victory against the favored Norwegian team in the first Women's World Championship in 1991.

By 1994, Michelle "had the world at my fingertips." But her success couldn't mask the fact that something was seriously wrong. After three years of battling extreme fatigue, she hit rock bottom—unable to get out of bed and brush her teeth, much less run and play aggressively on a soccer field.

Doctors diagnosed Chronic Fatigue Syndrome and pre-scribed a total lifestyle change. The effort she once concentrated on the soccer field now had to be applied to daily living. But in 1996, things took an upturn. She made radical changes to her diet, took an electrolyte replacement solution after workouts and gradually noticed she had more energy.

Pacing herself this time, she trained hard and got back into top form in time for the Olympic Games. Team USA took home the gold medal, and Michelle savored the triumph of a true comeback. "My teammates and I have given something to young female soccer players that we never had—someone to be like."

The most beautiful world is
always entered through the imagination.
If you wish to be something you are not—
something fine, noble, good—
you shut your eyes,
and for one dreamy
moment you are that
which you long to be.

HELEN KELLER

HELEN KELLER

Fueled by a fiery will and a lively imagination, Helen Keller was nonetheless trapped in a silent cocoon of darkness—the result of an illness that left her deaf and blind when she was a toddler. But in the end she attained her dream for far longer than a moment.

Captain Arthur and Kate Keller knew their firstborn was special—and very bright—when she managed to say "How d'ya do?" at age six months. According to her mother, she was almost running by her first birthday. But the joy of Helen's early childhood turned into a nightmare as the Kellers watched their young daughter fly into fits of rage, her only way to express the sense of helplessness she felt in her dark, silent world.

As Helen later wrote, "Gradually I got used to the silence and darkness that surrounded me and forgot that it had ever been different, until she came—my teacher—who was to set my spirit free. But during the first nineteen months of my life I had caught glimpses of broad, green fields, a luminous sky, trees and flowers, which the darkness that followed could not wholly blot out. If we have once seen, 'the day is ours, and what the day has shown.' "

"She" turned out to be Annie Sullivan, a feisty young Irish-woman who in 1887 traveled from Boston to Tuscumbia, Alabama, to be Helen's teacher. Annie immediately began spelling the name of objects into Helen's hand. To Helen, it was a wonderful new game, and she mimicked "Teacher's" hand movements. But the game was simply that to Helen: "I did not know that I was spelling a word, or even that words existed," she later recalled.

The breakthrough came one day as Annie placed Helen's hand under a water pump and spelled W-A-T-E-R into it, over and over. "I stood still, my whole attention fixed upon the motions of her fingers," Helen later wrote. "Suddenly I felt a misty consciousness as of something forgotten—a thrill of returning thought; and somehow the mystery of language was revealed to me. That living word awakened my soul, gave it light, hope, joy, set it free! There were barriers still, it is true, but barriers that could in time be swept away."

Through Annie's tireless tutoring, Helen went on to earn a degree from Radcliffe College in 1904, graduating cum laude and becoming the school's first blind student. After graduating, she dedicated herself to improving life for other people who were blind, lecturing and writing about her experiences in overcoming disabilities.

In *The Story of My Life,* Helen wrote: "In a thousand ways [my friends] have turned my limitations into beautiful privileges, and enabled me to walk serene and happy in the shadow cast by my deprivation."

The school of life offers
some difficult courses,
but it is in the difficult class
that one learns the most—
especially when your teacher
is the Lord Jesus Christ.

CORRIE TEN BOOM

CORRIE
TEN BOOM

For the first fifty years of her life, Corrie ten Boom lived a quiet life with her family above their watch shop in Haarlem, Holland. The narrow, creaking old house, three stories high, harbored not only their close-knit family but also the poor, the despised and the hunted of Haarlem during the early days of World War II. It also harbored a secret chamber—a hiding place for Jews hoping to escape the Nazi concentration camps.

Recalling the happy day in January 1937 that she, her father and her sister Betsie celebrated the watch shop's one hundredth anniversary, Corrie wrote in *The Hiding Place:* "How could we have guessed as we sat there. . .that in place of memories we were about to be given adventure such as we had never dreamed of? Adventure and anguish, horror and heaven were just around the corner, and we did not know. Oh Father! Betsie! If I had known would I have gone ahead? Could I have done the things I did?"

As the Nazis invaded Holland, the ten Boom family's open-door policy led to an elaborate "underground" operation that fed, clothed and housed Jews. When the Nazis discovered their scheme, Corrie and Betsie were shipped to a Dutch prison and eventually to the concentration camp at Ravensbruck.

Having smuggled a Bible into the prison camp, the sisters one by one ministered hope to their fellow prisoners. And even in the midst of Ravensbruck's horrors, a divine pattern began to emerge.

"God has plans—not problems—for our lives," writes Corrie in her book *Tramp for the Lord.* "Before she died in. . .Ravensbruck, my sister Betsie said to me, 'Corrie, your whole life has been a training for the work you are doing here in prison—and the work you will do afterward.' "

Upon her release from Ravensbruck—later found to be due to a "clerical" error—Corrie became a self-described "tramp for the Lord," traveling the globe with the story of salvation and Betsie's dream of opening a home for war victims.

One day, as she spoke at a church service in post-war Munich, she looked up and saw the former S.S. man who had stood guard at the shower room door at Ravensbruck. After her message, the man made his way to the front, thrust out his hand and said, "How grateful I am for your message, Fraulein. To think that, as you say, He has washed my sins away!"

Boiling with vengeful thoughts, Corrie breathed a silent prayer for supernatural forgiveness. As she took his hand, "the most incredible thing happened," she recalls. "From my shoulder along my arm and through my hand a current seemed to pass from me to him, while into my heart sprang a love for this stranger that almost overwhelmed me. And so I discovered that it is not on our forgiveness any more than on our goodness that the world's healing hinges, but on His. When He tells us to love our enemies, He gives, along with the command, the love itself."

My wonderful adventure that began as a young girl in China has no end in sight.
In fact, propelled by the everlasting love of God, it is on the threshold of its greatest beginning!

NORA LAM

N O R A
L A M

A loyal Communist believer and Party worker, Nora Lam studied hard to distinguish herself as a law student with a future in Chairman Mao's People's Republic of China.

It was 1953, still the early days of China's new regime. But signs of "cleansing" took place in the city streets with increasing regularity. Like the day Nora cycled home from classes and came upon an angry mob. Pushing her way into the throng, she saw two youths beating an elderly man, doubled up on the pavement. His crime: teaching the Christian Bible to young people.

Though she clung fiercely to the Revolution's ideals, Nora gazed at the now boarded-up churches of Shanghai as she pedaled toward home. A song from her childhood, learned at the McTyier Christian School, floated back to her across the years: "Jesus loves me, this I know. . . ." Two years later, working as a professor, she was brought in for questioning by Communist officials. Interrogated about her past—especially her attendance at two Christian schools—she reassured the officials that she no longer believed in the Christian God. Still suspicious, they required her to write out her life story, her "confession."

As she wrote, she recalled the night she had dedicated her life to God—but what she wrote was: "That experience from my childhood has no bearing on my life today in the new China."

Days passed, and the interrogations grew more intense—even cruel. Nora writes in her autobiography, *China Cry,* "I leaned against the desk trying to sleep. But I couldn't help again remembering the evening. . .when I accepted Christ as my Lord. Hot tears scalded my face and I whispered, 'I talked to You when I was a young girl. Do You remember my name?' "

Nora's next interrogation included physical beating.

"Are you a Christian?" the woman screamed. "Yes or no?"

"For an instant the temptation was strong," Nora recalls. *"Why not deny it? A dark voice seemed to whisper to me. After all, you believe in your heart, and God certainly knows. . ."*

Wiping the blood from her mouth, she thought of Jesus on the cross, blood trickling down His face. "He may be distant from me, but I will not deny His presence," she said.

The interrogator twitched with hate. "Answer me! Yes or no?"

"Yes! Oh, yes!" Nora cried out. "Yes, I am a Christian!"

Hauled outside to be shot, she breathed a prayer then awaited the bullets that would tear into her body. But as the shots rang out and chips of brick stung her back, she realized she had survived the firing squad.

Clinging to a promise from God that one day she and her entire family would escape from Red China, Nora eventually made it to Hong Kong and finally to the United States. Today she holds evangelistic crusades throughout the United States and China, pointing her listeners toward the One who gives hope against all odds.

"I find opportunities daily to. . .tell people how to be an overcomer and live a victorious life," she writes. "My wonderful adventure that began as a young girl in China has no end in sight. In fact, propelled by the everlasting love of God, it is on the threshold of its greatest beginning!"

In [perplexing] moments this is a most consoling thought: Only one thing at a time can be the will of God.

MARIA AUGUSTA TRAPP

MARIA
AUGUSTA TRAPP

At age twenty, Maria's demeanor befitted that of a young mountain goat more than a candidate for the novitiate at Nonnberg, the first Abbey of Benedictine Nuns north of the Alps. She took the stairs of the ancient edifice two and three at a time—and always got a gentle scolding for it.

Since candidates for the novitiate held the bottom rung of the abbey's hierarchy, the request to visit the Reverend Mother Abbess one day came as a surprise. Once inside the Reverend Mother's private parlor, the kind-faced older woman told Maria she must go to the house of a Baron von Trapp to teach his young daughter, who suffered from poor health. The teaching term would last only nine months, she was told. When it ended, she would return to the abbey.

"A few more words, a final blessing, and for the last time my fingers dipped into the pewter holy water font," Maria wrote in her autobiography, *The Story of the Trapp Family Singers.* "When I stepped from the cool archway into the centuries-old graveyard, my eyes. . .fell upon the inscription of a weathered gravestone, crooked with age: 'God's Will Hath No Why.' "

Turning for a last look at the abbey, she whispered, "I will be back—soon."

Once installed in the Villa Trapp—a gray, ivy-covered mansion—Maria fell in love with the former sea captain's seven children. The widowed captain, Georg von Trapp, seemed kind but aloof, and Maria saw a deep sadness in his eyes.

As the weeks flew by, Maria taught the children how to sing—and even how to play. Romping outdoors with their new governess, color came back into their once-pale cheeks.

When Maria heard that the captain intended to remarry, she added to her nightly prayers: "Dear Lord, send him a good wife who will be a good mother to his dear children, and let him be happy from now on."

Within a few months God answered her prayer, but not in the way she expected. After a cancelled engagement to an Austrian aristocrat, Georg asked Maria to be his wife instead.

As the Trapp family progressed in their music ability, invitations to play concerts poured in. Singing evenings at home turned into rehearsals. "Our hobby changed into a profession," Maria recalls. The family toured Europe, singing before kings and queens, in cathedrals and grand concert halls.

But casting a shadow over their joy was the dark threat of Hitler's Third Reich, which by March 1938 claimed Austria. Offered a tempting command over a Nazi submarine, Georg refused. Realizing the danger of saying no to the Fuhrer, he decided to take the family out of Austria at once. With the secret aid of their archbishop, the family escaped to England just one day before the border closed. From London, they boarded a ship bound for New York.

The family continued its singing career and eventually settled in Stowe, Vermont, on a hillside that reminded them of their Austrian home. "As the years go by," Maria wrote in 1949, "we see more and more that only one thing is necessary to be happy. . .and that one thing is not money, nor connections, nor health—it is love."

God doesn't need your intellect.
He doesn't need what you know
and how you know it.
He needs a vessel.
And when you get to the point where
you understand you're His vessel,
powerful things begin to happen.

BERNICE KING

B E R N I C E
K I N G

Growing up in the long shadow cast by her famous father, Bernice King struggled with her own identity and, later, outright anger toward God. By the time she was thirteen, four deaths had touched her immediate family, including the assassination of her father, Martin Luther King Jr., in 1968, and the murder of her grandmother.

"I was very angry at God," she recalls. "Angry at mother, angry at father, just angry at everybody. I literally grew up believing that death was after my family. I used to look at pictures of my family and try to figure out who was next." By the time she turned sixteen, "it had all just piled up."

Ironically, that anger became a turning point in her life. One year later, at seventeen, she says she heard the call of God on her life. Like her father, she knew she was destined to serve others in ministry. First, however, came an awakening of sorts.

While attending a youth retreat, Bernice watched a film titled *Montgomery to Memphis* along with the other teens. Nothing new here. She had seen the film dozens of times growing up.

But for some reason, this time when the film drew to a close, showing the scene of her father's funeral, she broke down.

"I ran out of the cabin and up into the woods," she recalls. "And for about two hours I just cried, asking why. Why he left. Why, God, did you take him? It was the first time I had grieved my father's death."

When the tears were spent, she fell quiet and realized she'd undergone a kind of cleansing. And with her grief came the maturity to face the future—but not necessarily her calling. It was fine for sometime off in the future, but not yet.

Opportunities to serve knocked early. She spoke at her church's Youth Day, became president of the youth ministry and held other leadership positions. But after college Bernice enrolled in a joint degree program of law and theology at Emory University, setting her sights on a career as a lawyer.

"I accepted the fact that I was going to theology school, but

I still did not accept my call," she remembers. "I knew I was going to have to accept it, because it was messing with me. But the more I ran the more the Lord kept speaking."

After a brush with death in an auto accident, Bernice says everything began to come into focus. In that crystallized moment, she realized God was with her—and that He had work for her to do.

On the eve of her twenty-fifth birthday, Bernice found herself sharing a heartfelt message to a full audience—the "official" beginning of her ministry. "I had peace about [the direction of my life]. But peace doesn't always mean you don't have questions, or that you don't have outside struggles," she says.

Today Bernice heads up a youth ministry at Atlanta's Greater Rising Star Baptist Church, and is often asked to speak in other venues. "Be true to who God called you to be," she says. "Don't fight the battle of trying to prove yourself. If you just be true to who God called you to be, He'll fight that battle."

It's a universal truth we all learned
in Sunday school.
"We are weak, but He is strong."
God always seems bigger to those
who need Him the most.

ℰ

JONI EARECKSON TADA

JONI
EARECKSON TADA

Paralyzed by a diving accident in 1967, Joni Eareckson found herself lying in a hospital bed with her head immobilized in steel tongs. It created a natural position for talking to God, she recalls —she was forced to stare straight at the ceiling.

"I tried to imagine what He was thinking," she wrote in her book *When God Weeps*. "A heavenly Father had to weep over me as my daddy often did, standing by my bedside, white-knuckling the guardrail. I was one of God's children, and God would never do anything to harm one of His own."

Once released from the hospital, friends drove Joni to Washington, D.C. to attend a service by a famous faith healer. Several services later, she sat in a line along with thirty other wheelchair-users waiting to exit the building, disappointed again.

Joni watched the people around her—confused people who had not received their healing. She realized that something was wrong, and began to question whether the best way to deal with suffering was to seek its immediate elimination.

Much as she suffered, Joni determined to live life to the fullest. During two grueling years of rehabilitation, she learned how to paint with a brush held between her teeth. When her paintings, and the story of her life, reached wide circulation, she became a sought-after motivational speaker and author. In time, she met and married Ken Tada, a high school teacher.

After ten years of her disability, Joni began to notice that all of her trials had strengthened her faith—made it "muscular," in her word. Her own suffering had made her sensitive to the needs of others, and really opened her eyes toward heavenly things, because "more is coming there."

Today, Joni heads up JAF Ministries (formerly Joni and Friends), an organization devoted to accelerating Christian ministry in the disability community. Through her work with JAF, she records a five-minute radio program heard on more than seven hundred broadcast outlets worldwide.

"Hardships press us up against God," she says of her life. And in the midst of those trials, "He gives us Himself."

No coward soul is mine,
No trembler in the world's
storm-troubled sphere:
I see Heaven's glories shine,
And faith shines equal,
arming me from fear.

EMILY BRONTË

Charm is deceptive and beauty is fleeting.
But a woman who fears the LORD
is to be praised.
Give her the reward she has earned,
and let her works bring her
praise at the city gate.

PROVERBS 31:30–31, NIV